BLUES PLAY-ALONG

ook & CD for B♭, E♭, Bass Clef and C instruments

VOLUME

7

Howlin' Wolf

PLAY 8 SONGS WITH A PROFESSIONAL BAND

HOW TO USE THE CD:

Each song has <u>two</u> tracks:

1) Full Stereo Mix

All recorded instruments are present on this track

2) Split Track

Piano and **Bass** parts can be removed
by turning down the volume on the LEFT channel.

Guitar and **Harmonica** parts can be removed
by turning down the volume on the RIGHT channel.

Cover photo © Sandy Guy Schoenfeld

ISBN 978-1-4234-8698-5

HAL•LEONARD® CORPORATION

7777 W. BLUEMOUND RD. P.O. BOX 13819 MILWAUKEE, WI 53213

Visit Hal Leonard Online at
www.halleonard.com

HOWLIN' WOLF

BOOK

TITLE	PAGE NUMBERS			
	C Treble Instruments	B♭ Instruments	E♭ Instruments	C Bass Instruments
Built for Comfort	4	20	36	52
Forty-Four	6	22	38	54
How Many More Years	8	24	40	56
Killing Floor	10	26	42	58
Moanin' at Midnight	12	28	44	60
Shake for Me	14	30	46	62
Sitting on Top of the World	16	32	48	64
Smokestack Lightning	18	34	50	66

CD

TITLE	CD Track Number Full Stereo Mix	CD Track Number Split Track
Built for Comfort	1	9
Forty-Four	2	10
How Many More Years	3	11
Killing Floor	4	12
Moanin' at Midnight	5	13
Shake for Me	6	14
Sitting on Top of the World	7	15
Smokestack Lightning	8	16

CD TRACK

1 Full Stereo Mix

9 Split Mix

C Version

Built for Comfort

Written by Willie Dixon

INTRO
MEDIUM SHUFFLE ♩ = 92

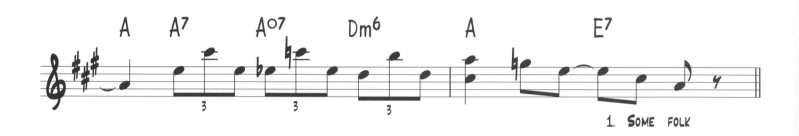

1. Some folk

.𝄋 VERSE

BUILT LIKE THIS, SOME FOLK BUILT LIKE THAT, A BUT THE
2., 3. See additional lyrics

WAY I'M BUILT A DON'T YOU CALL ME FAT. BE-CAUSE I'M

BUILT FOR COM-FORT, I _____ AIN'T BUILT FOR SPEED. _____

4

Additional Lyrics

2. Some folk rip and run, some folk believe in signs,
   But if you want me, baby, you got to take your time.
   Because I'm built for comfort, I ain't built for speed.
   But I got ev'rything, all the good girl needs.

3. I ain't got no diamonds, I ain't got no gold,
   But I do have love that's gonna fire your soul.
   Because I'm built for comfort, I ain't built for speed.
   But I got ev'rything, all you good women need.

C Version

Forty-Four
Words and Music by Chester Burnett

Intro
Moderate, double-time feel ♩ = 126

1. I wore my for-ty four so long, ___ I made my _
2. See additional lyrics

___ shoul-der sore. ___

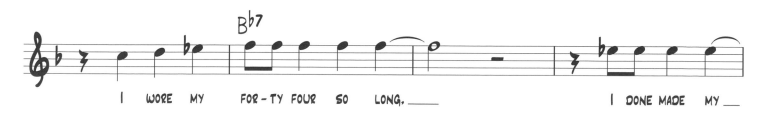

I wore my for-ty four so long, ___ I done made my ___

SHOUL-DER SORE.

WELL, I'M ___ GO-IN' MAD EV-'RY-BOD-Y, WHILE MY ___

BA-BY GONE.

SOLO

FINE

D.S. AL FINE

2. WELL, I'M SO

ADDITIONAL LYRICS

WELL, I'M SO MAD THIS MORNIN', I DON'T KNOW WHERE IN THE WORLD TO GO.
WELL, I'M SO MAD THIS MORNIN', I DON'T KNOW WHERE IN THE WORLD TO GO.
WELL, I'M LOOKIN' FIND ME SOME MONEY, PAWN GUN TO HAVE SOME GOLD.

How Many More Years

Words and Music by Chester Burnett

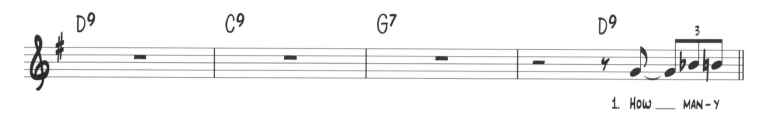

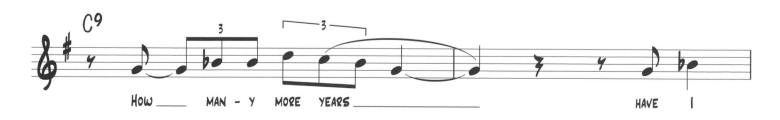

Additional Lyrics

2. I'm gonna fall on my knees, I'm gonna raise up my right hand.
   I'm gonna fall on my knees, I'm gonna raise up my right hand.
   Said, I feel much better darling, if you just only understand.

3. I'm goin' upstairs, I'm gonna bring back down my clothes.
   I'm goin' upstairs, I'm gonna bring back down my clothes.
   If anybody asks about me, just tell 'em I walked outdoors.

Killing Floor

Words and Music by Chester Burnett

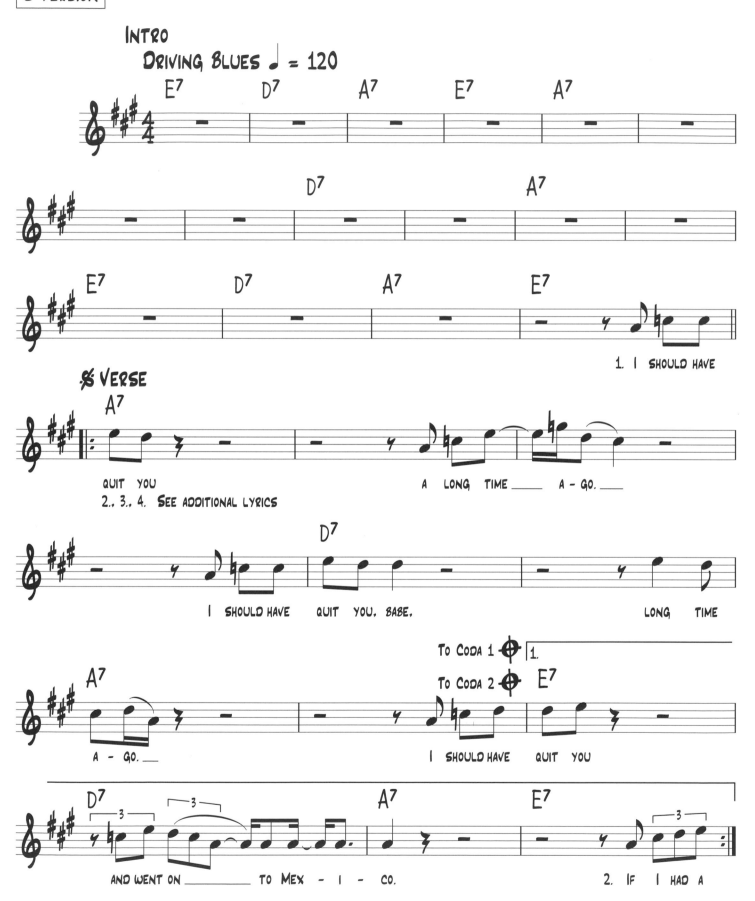

ADDITIONAL LYRICS

2. If I had a followed my first mind,
   If I had a followed my first mind,
   I'd a been gone since my second time.

3. I should have went on when my friend come from Mexico at me.
   I should have went on when my friend come from Mexico at me.
   But now I'm foolin' with you, baby, I let you put me on the killing floor.

4. God knows I should have been gone.
   God knows I should have been gone.
   Then I wouldn't have been here, down on the killing floor.

Moanin' at Midnight

Words and Music by Chester Burnett

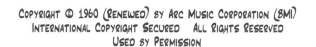

WHERE TO GO. __

2. WELL, ___ SOME - BOD - Y CALL - IN' ME, CALL - IN' ME

ON MY TEL-E - PHONE. ___

WELL, ___ SOME - BOD - Y CALL - IN' ME O - VER MY

TEL-E PHONE. __

WELL, KEEP ON CALL - IN' TELL 'EM __ I'M

NOT AT HOME. __

3. WELL, ___ DO NOT WOR - RY, DAD - DY IS GONE TO

BED. __

Shake for Me

Written by Willie Dixon

Intro
Medium Rock ♩ = 126

1. Sure ___

%. Verse

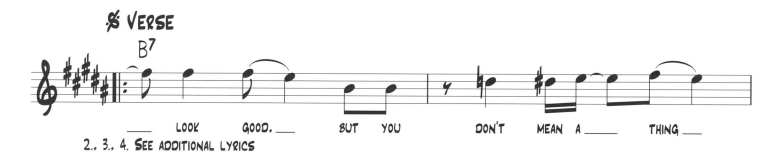

___ look good, ___ but you don't mean a ___ thing ___

2., 3., 4. See additional lyrics

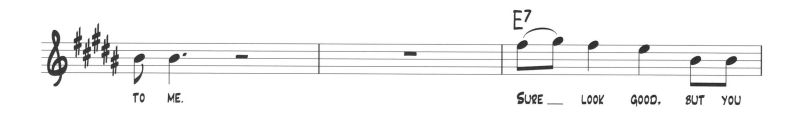

to me. Sure ___ look good, but you

don't mean a ___ thing ___ to me.

I GOT A HIP SHAK-IN' WOM-AN,   SHAKE LIKE A WIL-LOW

TREE.   2. YOU

GUITAR SOLO

D.S. AL CODA
(TAKE REPEAT)

CODA

3. WHEN MY

ADDITIONAL LYRICS

2. YOU WENT AWAY, BABY, YOU GOT BACK A LITTLE TOO LATE.
   YOU WENT AWAY, BABY, YOU GOT BACK A LITTLE TOO LATE.
   I GOT A COOL SHAKIN' BABY, SHAKE LIKE JELL-O ON A PLATE.

3. WHEN MY BABY WALK, YOU KNOW SHE'S FINE AND MELLOW.
   WHEN MY BABY WALK, YOU KNOW SHE'S FINE AND MELLOW.
   EVERY TIME SHE STOP, HER FLESH IT SHAKE LIKE JELL-O.

4. OH, SHAKE IT, BABY, SHAKE IT FOR ME.
   OH, SHAKE IT, LITTLE BABY, SHAKE IT FOR ME.
   OH, SHAKE IT, LITTLE BABY, JUST SHAKE LIKE A WILLOW TREE.

Sitting on Top of the World

Words and Music by Chester Burnett

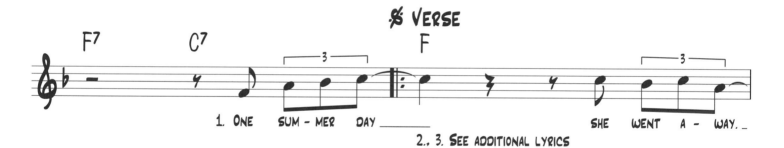

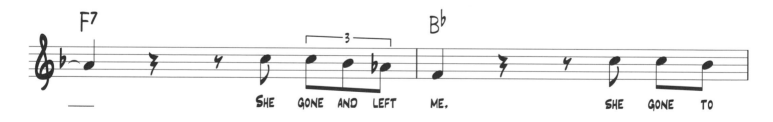

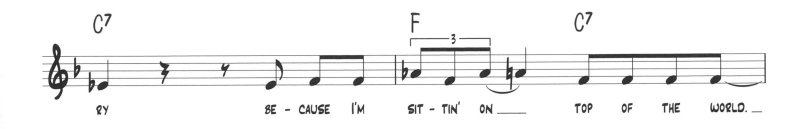

RY — BE - CAUSE I'M SIT - TIN' ON ___ TOP OF THE WORLD. ___

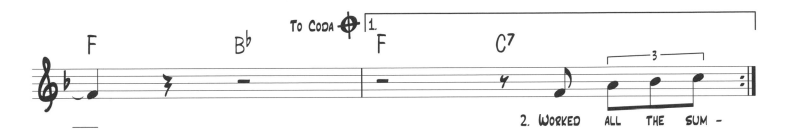

To Coda ⊕ 1.

___   2. Worked all the sum -

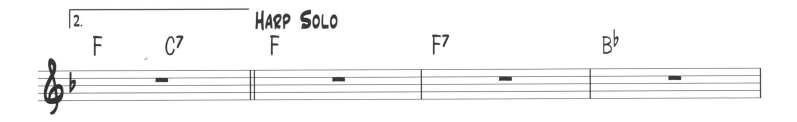

2.   Harp Solo

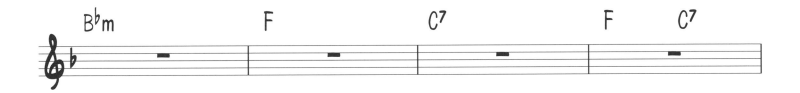

D.S. al Coda   ⊕ Coda

3. Goin' down to the freight

Additional Lyrics

2. Worked all the summer, worked all the fall.
    Had to take Christmas in my overalls.
    But now she's gone, and I don't worry.
    Sittin' on top of the world.

3. Goin' down to the freight yard, catch me a freight train.
    I'm gonna leave this town, work done got hard.
    But now she's gone, and I don't worry.
    Sittin' on top of the world.

C Version

Smokestack Lightning

Words and Music by Chester Burnett

Intro
Medium fast, half-time feel ♩ = 144

Verse

1. Oh oh, ____ smoke-stack light - nin', ____ shin - in' ____
3., 5. See additional lyrics

just like gold. Oh, don't you hear ____ me cry - ing? Woo - ooh. ____

____ Woo - ooh. _____ Woo - ooh.

VERSE

2. Oh, oh, _____ tell me ba - by, what's the ___
4., 6. See additional lyrics

mat - ter here? Oh, don't you hear _____ me cry - ing?

Woo - ooh. _____ Woo - ooh. _____

HARP SOLO

Woo - ooh.

1., 2.   3.   **OUTRO-HARP SOLO**

Additional Lyrics

3. Whoa, oh tell me baby, where did you stay last night?
   Oh don't you hear me crying? Woo-ooh. Woo-ooh. Woo-ooh.

4. Whoa, oh stop your train, let a poor boy ride.
   Whoa, don't you hear me crying? Woo-ooh. Woo-ooh. Woo-ooh.

5. Whoa, oh fare you well, never see you no more.
   Oh don't you hear me crying? Woo-ooh. Woo-ooh. Woo-ooh.

6. Oh, oh, who been here, baby, since I been gone?
   Little bitty boy with a derby on. Woo-ooh. Woo-ooh. Woo-ooh.

CD TRACK

1 Full Stereo Mix
9 Split Mix

Bb Version

Built for Comfort
Written by Willie Dixon

Intro
Medium Shuffle ♩ = 92

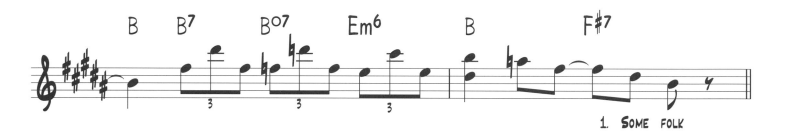

1. Some folk

 Verse

Built like this, some folk built like that, a but the
2., 3. See additional lyrics

way I'm built a don't you call me fat. Be-cause I'm

Built for com-fort, I ain't built for speed.

Additional Lyrics

2. Some folk rip and run, some folk believe in signs,
But if you want me, baby, you got to take your time.
Because I'm built for comfort, I ain't built for speed.
But I got ev'rything, all the good girl needs.

3. I ain't got no diamonds, I ain't got no gold,
But I do have love that's gonna fire your soul.
Because I'm built for comfort, I ain't built for speed.
But I got ev'rything, all you good women need.

Forty-Four

Words and Music by Chester Burnett

Intro
Moderate, double-time feel ♩ = 126

%. Verse

1. I wore my for-ty four so long, ___ I made my _

2. See additional lyrics

___ shoul-der sore. ___

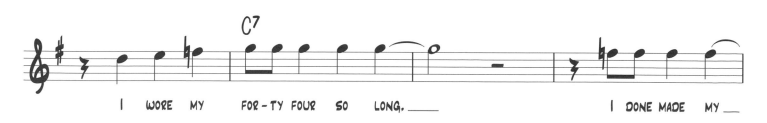

I wore my for-ty four so long, ___ I done made my ___

SHOUL-DER SORE.

WELL, I'M GO-IN' MAD EV-'RY-BOD-Y, WHILE MY

BA-BY GONE.

FINE

SOLO

D.S. AL FINE

2. WELL, I'M SO

ADDITIONAL LYRICS

WELL, I'M SO MAD THIS MORNIN', I DON'T KNOW WHERE IN THE WORLD TO GO.
WELL, I'M SO MAD THIS MORNIN', I DON'T KNOW WHERE IN THE WORLD TO GO.
WELL, I'M LOOKIN' FIND ME SOME MONEY, PAWN GUN TO HAVE SOME GOLD.

How Many More Years
Words and Music by Chester Burnett

Additional Lyrics

2. I'm gonna fall on my knees, I'm gonna raise up my right hand.
I'm gonna fall on my knees, I'm gonna raise up my right hand.
Said, I feel much better darling, if you just only understand.

3. I'm goin' upstairs, I'm gonna bring back down my clothes.
I'm goin' upstairs, I'm gonna bring back down my clothes.
If anybody asks about me, just tell 'em I walked outdoors.

CD TRACK
◆4 Full Stereo Mix
◆12 Split Mix

B♭ Version

Killing Floor

Words and Music by Chester Burnett

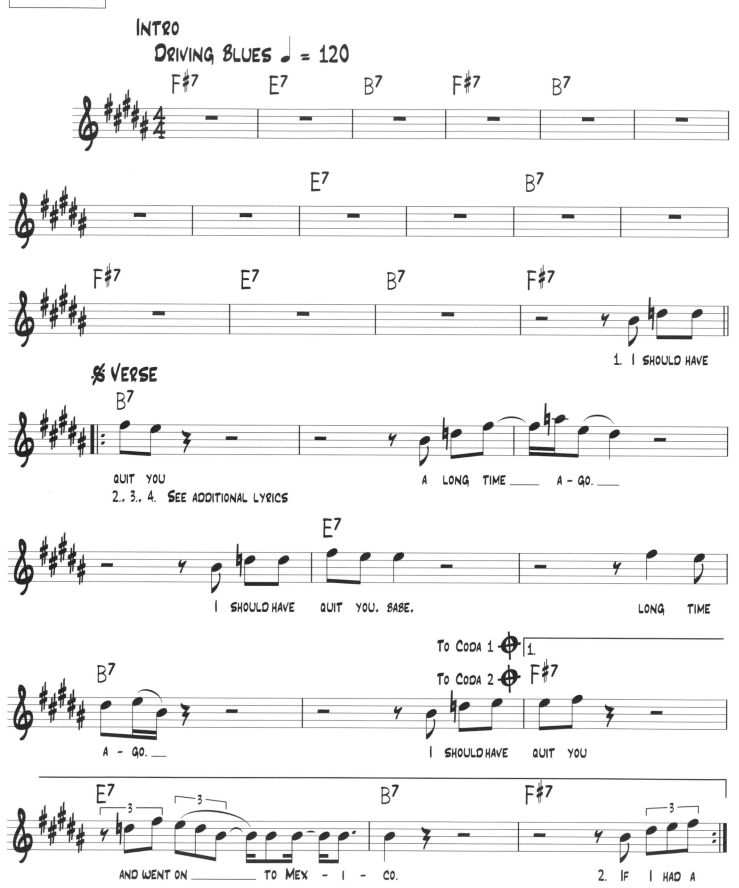

INTRO
DRIVING BLUES ♩ = 120

Lyrics in score:
1. I should have quit you
2., 3., 4. See additional lyrics
A long time a-go.
I should have quit you, babe, long time a-go.
I should have quit you
and went on to Mex-i-co.
2. If I had a

Additional Lyrics

2. If I had a followed my first mind,
   If I had a followed my first mind,
   I'd a been gone since my second time.

3. I should have went on when my friend come from Mexico at me.
   I should have went on when my friend come from Mexico at me.
   But now I'm foolin' with you, baby, I let you put me on the killing floor.

4. God knows I should have been gone.
   God knows I should have been gone.
   Then I wouldn't have been here, down on the killing floor.

Moanin' At Midnight

Words and Music by Chester Burnett

INTRO
TWO-BEAT FEEL ♩ = 88

VERSE

1. There's _____ some - bod - y

knock - in' on my door. _____

There's _____ some - bod - y

knock - in' on my door. _____

Well, I'm so wor - ried don't know

WHERE TO GO.

2. WELL, SOME - BOD-Y CALL - IN' ME. CALL - IN' ME

ON MY TEL-E - PHONE.

WELL, SOME - BOD-Y CALL - IN' ME O - VER MY

TEL-E - PHONE.

WELL, KEEP ON CALL - IN' TELL 'EM I'M

NOT AT HOME.

3. WELL, DO NOT WOR - RY, DAD - DY IS GONE TO

BED.

CD TRACK
6 Full Stereo Mix
14 Split Mix

8♭ Version

Shake for Me
Written by Willie Dixon

Intro
Medium Rock ♩ = 126

1. Sure ___

___ look good. ___ but you don't mean a ___ thing ___

2., 3., 4. See additional lyrics

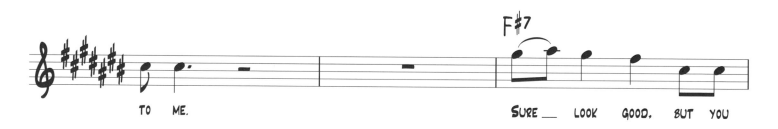

to me.   Sure ___ look good. but you

don't mean a ___ thing ___ to me.

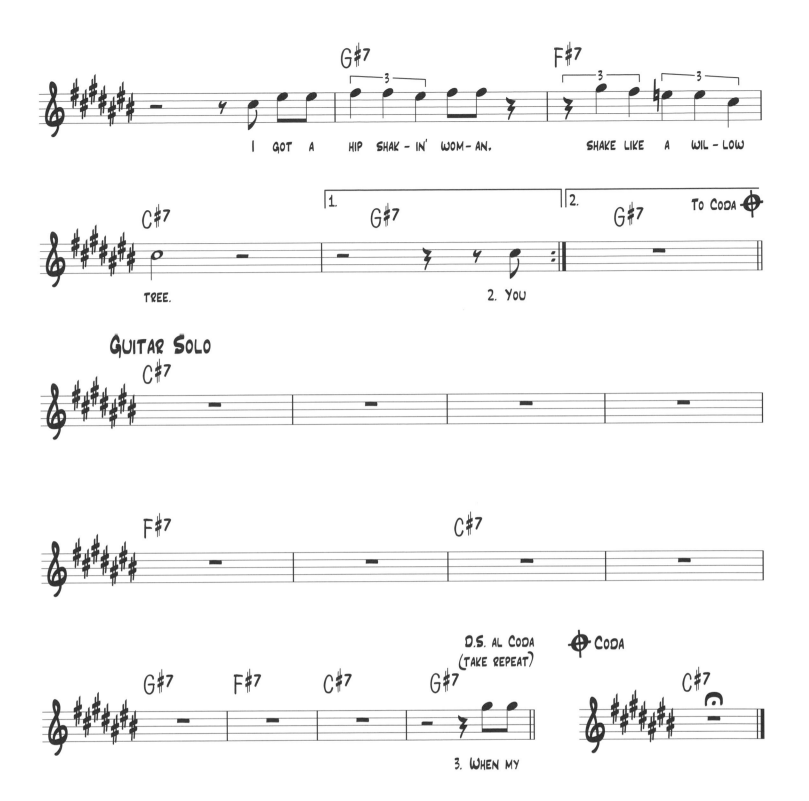

I GOT A HIP SHAK-IN' WOM-AN, SHAKE LIKE A WIL-LOW TREE.

2. YOU

GUITAR SOLO

D.S. AL CODA
(TAKE REPEAT)

3. WHEN MY

ADDITIONAL LYRICS

2. YOU WENT AWAY, BABY, YOU GOT BACK A LITTLE TOO LATE.
   YOU WENT AWAY, BABY, YOU GOT BACK A LITTLE TOO LATE.
   I GOT A COOL SHAKIN' BABY, SHAKE LIKE JELL-O ON A PLATE.

3. WHEN MY BABY WALK, YOU KNOW SHE'S FINE AND MELLOW.
   WHEN MY BABY WALK, YOU KNOW SHE'S FINE AND MELLOW.
   EVERY TIME SHE STOP, HER FLESH IT SHAKE LIKE JELL-O.

4. OH, SHAKE IT, BABY, SHAKE IT FOR ME.
   OH, SHAKE IT, LITTLE BABY, SHAKE IT FOR ME.
   OH, SHAKE IT, LITTLE BABY, JUST SHAKE LIKE A WILLOW TREE.

Sitting on Top of the World

Words and Music by Chester Burnett

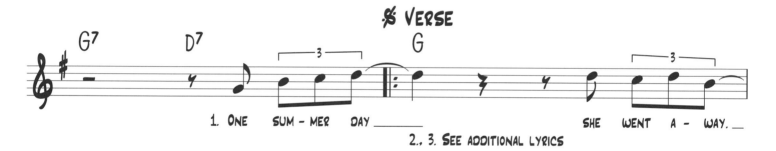

1. One sum-mer day _____ She went a - way. _____
2., 3. See additional lyrics

She gone and left me, she gone to

stay. But now she's gone, and I can't wor-

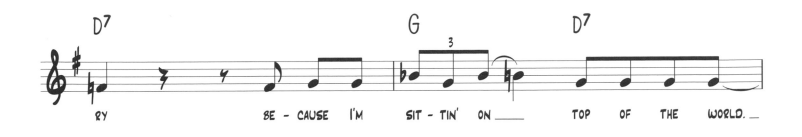

RY BE - CAUSE I'M SIT - TIN' ON ____ TOP OF THE WORLD. ____

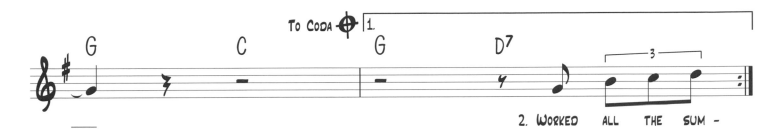

____ 2. WORKED ALL THE SUM -

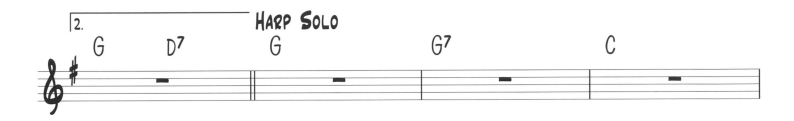

HARP SOLO

D.S. AL CODA   CODA

3. GOIN' DOWN TO THE FREIGHT

ADDITIONAL LYRICS

2. WORKED ALL THE SUMMER, WORKED ALL THE FALL.
   HAD TO TAKE CHRISTMAS IN MY OVERALLS.
   BUT NOW SHE'S GONE, AND I DON'T WORRY.
   SITTIN' ON TOP OF THE WORLD.

3. GOIN' DOWN TO THE FREIGHT YARD, CATCH ME A FREIGHT TRAIN.
   I'M GONNA LEAVE THIS TOWN, WORK DONE GOT HARD.
   BUT NOW SHE'S GONE, AND I DON'T WORRY.
   SITTIN' ON TOP OF THE WORLD.

Bb Version

Smokestack Lightning

Words and Music by Chester Burnett

INTRO
Medium fast, half-time feel ♩ = 144

1. Oh oh, _____ smoke-stack light - nin', shin - in' ___
3., 5. See additional lyrics

just like gold. Oh, don't you hear ___ me cry - ing? Woo - ooh.

___ Woo - ooh. _____ Woo - ooh.

Additional Lyrics

3. Whoa, oh tell me baby, where did you stay last night?
   Oh don't you hear me crying? Woo-ooh. Woo-ooh. Woo-ooh.

4. Whoa, oh stop your train, let a poor boy ride.
   Whoa, don't you hear me crying? Woo-ooh. Woo-ooh. Woo-ooh.

5. Whoa, oh fare you well, never see you no more.
   Oh don't you hear me crying? Woo-ooh. Woo-ooh. Woo-ooh.

6. Oh, oh, who been here, baby, since I been gone?
   Little bitty boy with a derby on. Woo-ooh. Woo-ooh. Woo-ooh.

Eb Version

Built for Comfort
Written by Willie Dixon

Intro
Medium Shuffle ♩ = 92

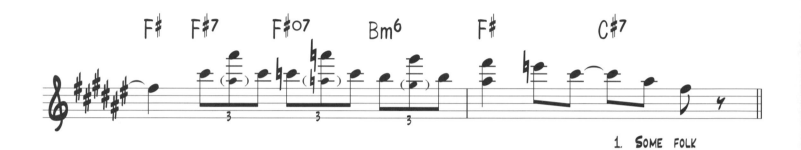

1. Some folk

$\mathbf{\%}$ Verse

BUILT LIKE THIS,   SOME FOLK   BUILT LIKE THAT,   A   BUT THE
2., 3. See additional lyrics

WAY I'M BUILT   A   DON'T YOU   CALL   ME   FAT.   BE - CAUSE I'M

BUILT FOR COM - FORT.   I _____ AIN'T BUILT FOR SPEED. __

BUT I GOT EV - 'RY - THING. ___

ALL ___ THAT A GOOD GIRL NEEDS. ___

2. SOME FOLK

GUITAR SOLO

3. I ___ AIN'T

ADDITIONAL LYRICS

2. SOME FOLK RIP AND RUN, SOME FOLK BELIEVE IN SIGNS,
BUT IF YOU WANT ME, BABY, YOU GOT TO TAKE YOUR TIME.
BECAUSE I'M BUILT FOR COMFORT, I AIN'T BUILT FOR SPEED.
BUT I GOT EV'RYTHING, ALL THE GOOD GIRL NEEDS.

3. I AIN'T GOT NO DIAMONDS, I AIN'T GOT NO GOLD,
BUT I DO HAVE LOVE THAT'S GONNA FIRE YOUR SOUL.
BECAUSE I'M BUILT FOR COMFORT, I AIN'T BUILT FOR SPEED.
BUT I GOT EV'RYTHING, ALL YOU GOOD WOMEN NEED.

Forty-Four

Words and Music by Chester Burnett

Intro
Moderate, double-time feel ♩ = 126

1. I wore my for-ty four so long, ___ I made my ___
2. See additional lyrics

___ shoul-der sore. ___

I wore my for-ty four so long, ___ I done made my ___

SHOUL-DER SORE.

WELL, I'M __ GO-IN' MAD EV-'RY-BOD-Y, WHILE MY __

BA-BY GONE.

SOLO

ADDITIONAL LYRICS

WELL, I'M SO MAD THIS MORNIN', I DON'T KNOW WHERE IN THE WORLD TO GO.
WELL, I'M SO MAD THIS MORNIN', I DON'T KNOW WHERE IN THE WORLD TO GO.
WELL, I'M LOOKIN' FIND ME SOME MONEY, PAWN GUN TO HAVE SOME GOLD.

How Many More Years

Words and Music by Chester Burnett

GOT TO LET YOU DOG___ ME A - ROUND?

3RD X TO CODA

I'D AS SOON ___ RATH - ER BE DEAD. ___ SLEEP - IN' SIX ___

___ FEET IN THE GROUND. ___

HARP SOLO

2. I'M ___ GON - NA

3. I'M ___ GOIN' ___

D.S. AL CODA

CODA

JUST TELL 'EM I WALKED OUT - DOORS.

ADDITIONAL LYRICS

2. I'M GONNA FALL ON MY KNEES, I'M GONNA RAISE UP MY RIGHT HAND.
   I'M GONNA FALL ON MY KNEES, I'M GONNA RAISE UP MY RIGHT HAND.
   SAID, I FEEL MUCH BETTER DARLING, IF YOU JUST ONLY UNDERSTAND.

3. I'M GOIN' UPSTAIRS, I'M GONNA BRING BACK DOWN MY CLOTHES.
   I'M GOIN' UPSTAIRS, I'M GONNA BRING BACK DOWN MY CLOTHES.
   IF ANYBODY ASKS ABOUT ME, JUST TELL 'EM I WALKED OUTDOORS.

Killing Floor
Words and Music by Chester Burnett

E♭ Version

Intro
Driving Blues ♩ = 120

1. I should have

Verse

quit you
2., 3., 4. See additional lyrics

a long time ___ a-go. ___

I should have quit you, babe,   long   time

To Coda 1
To Coda 2

a-go. ___   I should have quit you

and went on ___ to Mex-i-co.   2. If I had a

Additional Lyrics

2. IF I HAD A FOLLOWED MY FIRST MIND,
   IF I HAD A FOLLOWED MY FIRST MIND,
   I'D A BEEN GONE SINCE MY SECOND TIME.

3. I SHOULD HAVE WENT ON WHEN MY FRIEND COME FROM MEXICO AT ME.
   I SHOULD HAVE WENT ON WHEN MY FRIEND COME FROM MEXICO AT ME.
   BUT NOW I'M FOOLIN' WITH YOU, BABY, I LET YOU PUT ME ON THE KILLING FLOOR.

4. GOD KNOWS I SHOULD HAVE BEEN GONE.
   GOD KNOWS I SHOULD HAVE BEEN GONE.
   THEN I WOULDN'T HAVE BEEN HERE, DOWN ON THE KILLING FLOOR.

Moanin' at Midnight
Words and Music by Chester Burnett

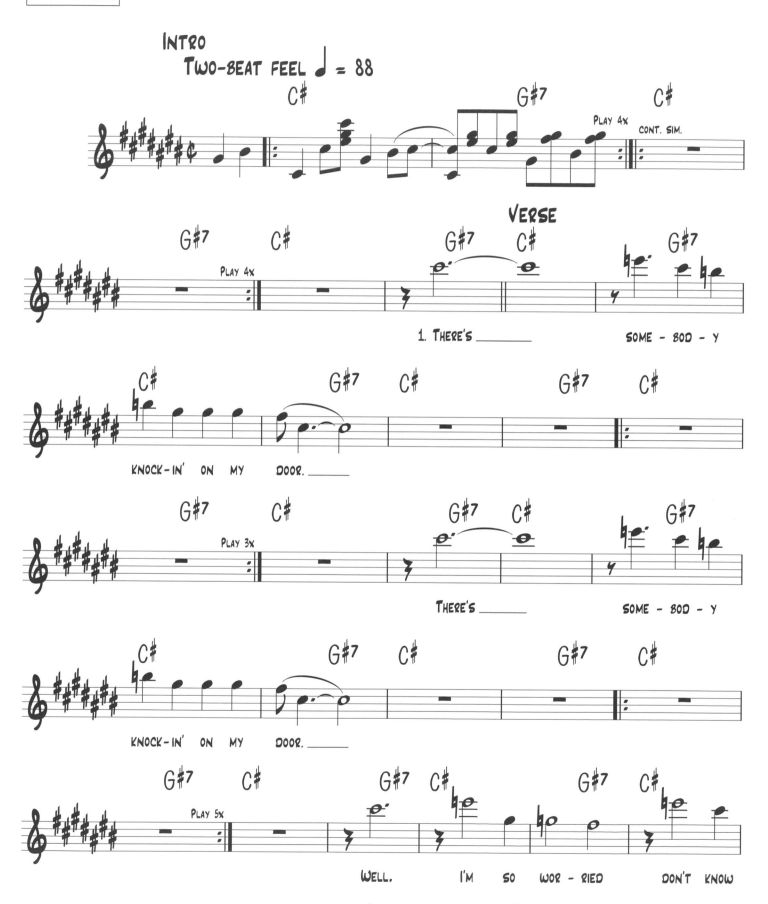

CD TRACK
6 Full Stereo Mix
14 Split Mix

Eb Version

Shake for Me
Written by Willie Dixon

1. Sure ___

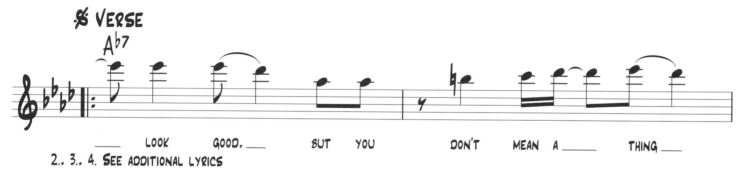

___ ___ LOOK GOOD, ___ BUT YOU DON'T MEAN A ___ THING ___

2., 3., 4. See additional lyrics

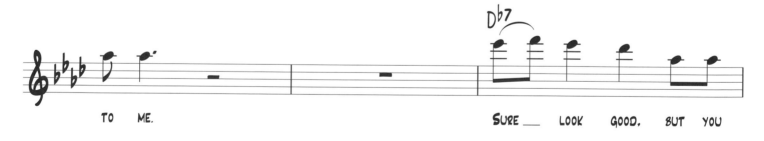

TO ME. SURE ___ LOOK GOOD, BUT YOU

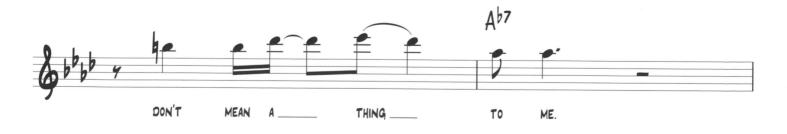

DON'T MEAN A ___ THING ___ TO ME.

Additional Lyrics

2. You went away, baby, you got back a little too late.
   You went away, baby, you got back a little too late.
   I got a cool shakin' baby, shake like Jell-o on a plate.

3. When my baby walk, you know she's fine and mellow.
   When my baby walk, you know she's fine and mellow.
   Every time she stop, her flesh it shake like Jell-o.

4. Oh, shake it, baby, shake it for me.
   Oh, shake it, little baby, shake it for me.
   Oh, shake it, little baby, just shake like a willow tree.

CD TRACK

7 Full Stereo Mix

15 Split Mix

Eb Version

Sitting on Top of the World
Words and Music by Chester Burnett

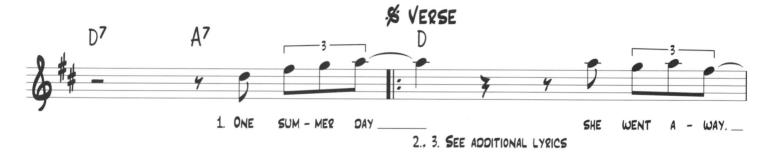

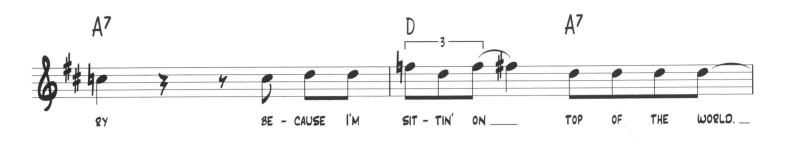

RY   BE - CAUSE I'M   SIT - TIN' ON _____ TOP OF THE WORLD. _____

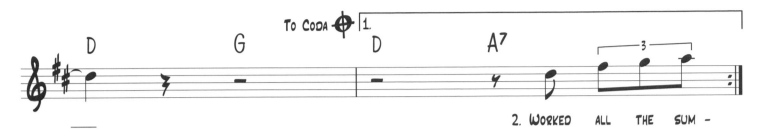

2. WORKED ALL THE SUM -

HARP SOLO

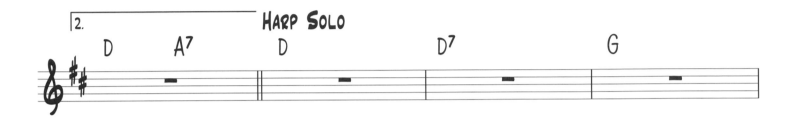

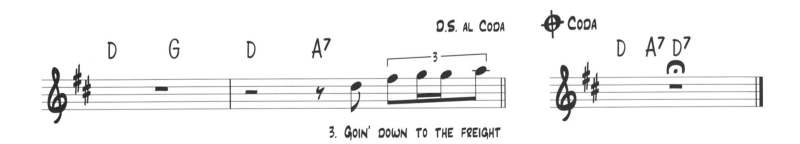

3. GOIN' DOWN TO THE FREIGHT

ADDITIONAL LYRICS

2. Worked all the summer, worked all the fall.
   Had to take Christmas in my overalls.
   But now she's gone, and I don't worry.
   Sittin' on top of the world.

3. Goin' down to the freight yard, catch me a freight train.
   I'm gonna leave this town, work done got hard.
   But now she's gone, and I don't worry.
   Sittin' on top of the world.

Smokestack Lightning

Words and Music by Chester Burnett

Intro
Medium fast, half-time feel ♩ = 144

Verse

1. Oh oh, _____ smoke-stack light - nin', shin - in' ___
3., 5. See additional lyrics

Just like gold. Oh, don't you hear ___ me cry - ing? Woo-ooh.

___ Woo-ooh. _____ Woo - ooh.

50

Additional Lyrics

3. Whoa, oh tell me baby, where did you stay last night?
   Oh don't you hear me crying? Woo-ooh. Woo-ooh. Woo-ooh.

4. Whoa, oh stop your train, let a poor boy ride.
   Whoa, don't you hear me crying? Woo-ooh. Woo-ooh. Woo-ooh.

5. Whoa, oh fare you well, never see you no more.
   Oh don't you hear me crying? Woo-ooh. Woo-ooh. Woo-ooh.

6. Oh, oh, who been here, baby, since I been gone?
   Little bitty boy with a derby on. Woo-ooh. Woo-ooh. Woo-ooh.

① Full Stereo Mix
⑨ Split Mix

C Version

Built for Comfort
Written by Willie Dixon

Intro
Medium Shuffle ♩ = 92

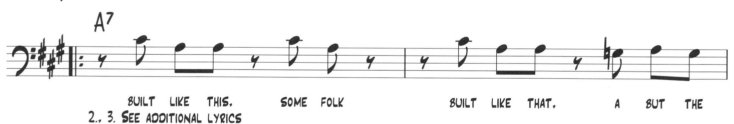

1. Some folk

Verse

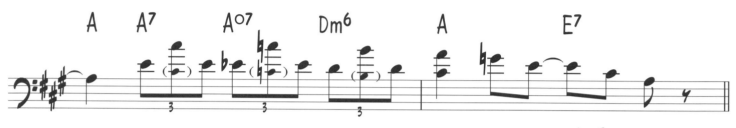

Built like this, some folk built like that, a but the
2., 3. See additional lyrics

way I'm built a don't you call me fat. Be - cause I'm

Built for com - fort, I _____ ain't built for speed. ___

BUT I GOT EV-'RY-THING. ___

ALL _____ THAT A GOOD GIRL NEEDS. ___

2. SOME FOLK

3. I ___ AIN'T ___

ADDITIONAL LYRICS

2. SOME FOLK RIP AND RUN, SOME FOLK BELIEVE IN SIGNS,
   BUT IF YOU WANT ME, BABY, YOU GOT TO TAKE YOUR TIME.
   BECAUSE I'M BUILT FOR COMFORT, I AIN'T BUILT FOR SPEED.
   BUT I GOT EV'RYTHING, ALL THE GOOD GIRL NEEDS.

3. I AIN'T GOT NO DIAMONDS, I AIN'T GOT NO GOLD,
   BUT I DO HAVE LOVE THAT'S GONNA FIRE YOUR SOUL.
   BECAUSE I'M BUILT FOR COMFORT, I AIN'T BUILT FOR SPEED.
   BUT I GOT EV'RYTHING, ALL YOU GOOD WOMEN NEED.

FORTY-FOUR
WORDS AND MUSIC BY CHESTER BURNETT

INTRO
MODERATE, DOUBLE-TIME FEEL ♩ = 126

1. I WORE MY   FOR-TY FOUR SO   LONG. ___   I MADE MY _
2. SEE ADDITIONAL LYRICS

___ SHOUL-DER   SORE. ___

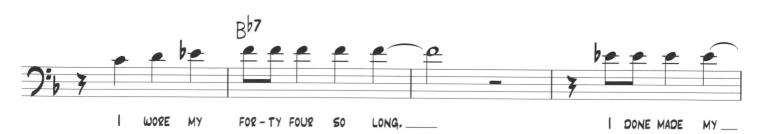

I   WORE   MY   FOR-TY FOUR   SO   LONG, ___   I DONE MADE   MY ___

SHOUL - DER SORE.

WELL, I'M ___ GO - IN' MAD EV - 'RY - BOD - Y, WHILE MY ___

BA - BY GONE. ___

Solo

2. WELL, I'M SO

Additional Lyrics

Well, I'm so mad this mornin', I don't know where in the world to go.
Well, I'm so mad this mornin', I don't know where in the world to go.
Well, I'm lookin' find me some money, pawn gun to have some gold.

How Many More Years
Words and Music by Chester Burnett

Intro
Medium Shuffle ♩ = 120

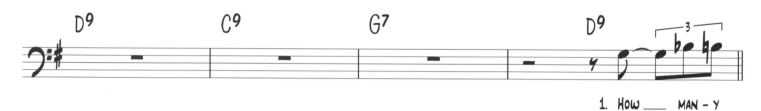

1. How ___ man - y

.𝄈 VERSE

more years ___
2., 3., See additional lyrics
HAVE I GOT TO LET YOU DOG ___

___ me a - round?

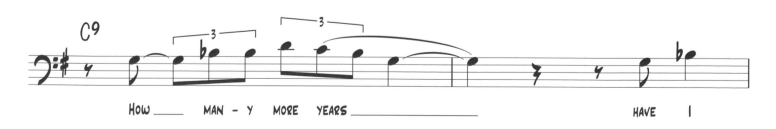

How ___ man - y more years ___ have I

GOT TO LET YOU DOG___ ME A - ROUND?

I'D AS SOON___ RATH - ER BE DEAD, ___ SLEEP - IN' SIX___

___ FEET IN THE GROUND. ___

Harp Solo

2. I'M ___ GON - NA

3. I'M ___ GOIN' ___

JUST TELL 'EM I WALKED OUT - DOORS.

Additional Lyrics

2. I'M GONNA FALL ON MY KNEES, I'M GONNA RAISE UP MY RIGHT HAND.
   I'M GONNA FALL ON MY KNEES, I'M GONNA RAISE UP MY RIGHT HAND.
   SAID, I FEEL MUCH BETTER DARLING, IF YOU JUST ONLY UNDERSTAND.

3. I'M GOIN' UPSTAIRS, I'M GONNA BRING BACK DOWN MY CLOTHES.
   I'M GOIN' UPSTAIRS, I'M GONNA BRING BACK DOWN MY CLOTHES.
   IF ANYBODY ASKS ABOUT ME, JUST TELL 'EM I WALKED OUTDOORS.

Killing Floor

Words and Music by Chester Burnett

Additional Lyrics

2. If I had a followed my first mind.
   If I had a followed my first mind.
   I'd a been gone since my second time.

3. I should have went on when my friend come from Mexico at me.
   I should have went on when my friend come from Mexico at me.
   But now I'm foolin' with you, baby, I let you put me on the killing floor.

4. God knows I should have been gone.
   God knows I should have been gone.
   Then I wouldn't have been here, down on the killing floor.

Moanin' At Midnight
Words and Music by Chester Burnett

61

CD TRACK

◆ 6 Full Stereo Mix

◆ 14 Split Mix

𝄢 C Version

Shake for Me

Written by Willie Dixon

Intro
Medium Rock ♩ = 126

1. Sure ___

%. Verse

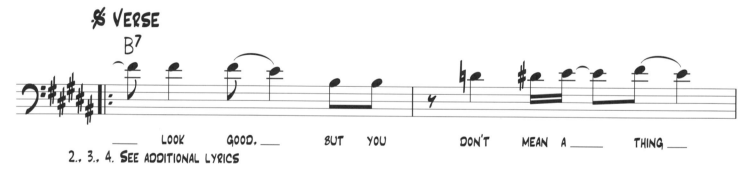

___ look good, ___ but you don't mean a ___ thing ___
2., 3., 4. See additional lyrics

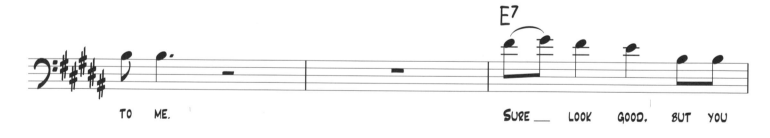

to me.   Sure ___ look good, but you

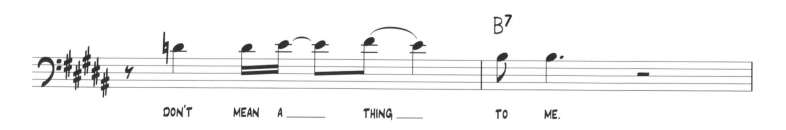

don't mean a ___ thing ___ to me.

CD TRACK

7 Full Stereo Mix

15 Split Mix

𝄢 C Version

Sitting on Top of the World

Words and Music by Chester Burnett

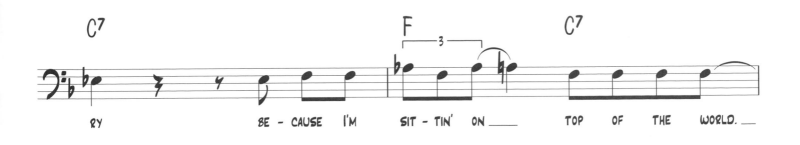

RY — BE - CAUSE I'M SIT - TIN' ON ____ TOP OF THE WORLD. ___

To Coda ⊕ | 1. F — C⁷

___ 2. Worked all the sum -

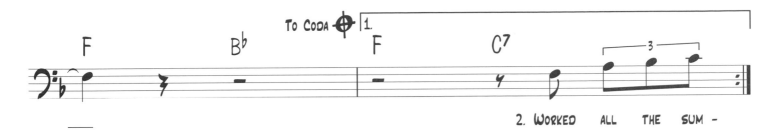

| 2. | Harp Solo |

D.S. al Coda ⊕ Coda

3. Goin' down to the freight

Additional Lyrics

2. Worked all the summer, worked all the fall.
   Had to take Christmas in my overalls.
   But now she's gone, and I don't worry.
   Sittin' on top of the world.

3. Goin' down to the freight yard, catch me a freight train.
   I'm gonna leave this town, work done got hard.
   But now she's gone, and I don't worry.
   Sittin' on top of the world.

Smokestack Lightning

Words and Music by Chester Burnett

Intro
Medium fast, half-time feel ♩ = 144

Verse

1. Oh   oh,_____ smoke-stack light - nin',   shin - in'___
3., 5. See additional lyrics

just like gold.   Oh, don't you hear ____ me cry - ing?   Woo - ooh. _____

_____   Woo - ooh. _____   Woo - ooh.

Additional Lyrics

3. Whoa, oh tell me baby, where did you stay last night?
   Oh don't you hear me crying? Woo-ooh. Woo-ooh. Woo-ooh.

4. Whoa, oh stop your train, let a poor boy ride.
   Whoa, don't you hear me crying? Woo-ooh. Woo-ooh. Woo-ooh.

5. Whoa, oh fare you well, never see you no more.
   Oh don't you hear me crying? Woo-ooh. Woo-ooh. Woo-ooh.

6. Oh, oh, who been here, baby, since I been gone?
   Little bitty boy with a derby on. Woo-ooh. Woo-ooh. Woo-ooh.

THE ULTIMATE COLLECTION OF
FAKE BOOKS

The Real Book – Sixth Edition

Hal Leonard proudly presents the first legitimate and legal editions of these books ever produced. These bestselling titles are mandatory for anyone who plays jazz! Over 400 songs, including: All By Myself • Dream a Little Dream of Me • God Bless the Child • Like Someone in Love • When I Fall in Love • and more.

00240221 Volume 1, C Edition $29.99
00240224 Volume 1, B♭ Edition $29.99
00240225 Volume 1, E♭ Edition $29.99
00240226 Volume 1, BC Edition $29.95
00240222 Volume 2, C Edition $29.95
00240227 Volume 2, B♭ Edition $29.95
00240228 Volume 2, E♭ Edition $29.95

Best Fake Book Ever – 3rd Edition

More than 1,000 songs from all styles of music, including: All My Loving • At the Hop • Cabaret • Dust in the Wind • Fever • From a Distance • Hello, Dolly! • Hey Jude • King of the Road • Longer • Misty • Route 66 • Sentimental Journey • Somebody • Song Sung Blue • Spinning Wheel • Unchained Melody • We Will Rock You • What a Wonderful World • Wooly Bully • Y.M.C.A. • and more.

00290239 C Edition $49.99
00240083 B♭ Edition $49.95
00240084 E♭ Edition $49.95

Classic Rock Fake Book – 2nd Edition

This fake book is a great compilation of more than 250 terrific songs of the rock era, arranged for piano, voice, guitar and all C instruments. Includes: All Right Now • American Woman • Birthday • Honesty • I Shot the Sheriff • I Want You to Want Me • Imagine • It's Still Rock and Roll to Me • Lay Down Sally • Layla • My Generation • Rock and Roll All Nite • Spinning Wheel • White Room • We Will Rock You • lots more!

00240108 ....$29.95

Classical Fake Book – 2nd Edition

This unprecedented, amazingly comprehensive reference includes over 850 classical themes and melodies for all classical music lovers. Includes everything from Renaissance music to Vivaldi and Mozart to Mendelssohn. Lyrics in the original language are included when appropriate.

00240044 ....$34.95

The Disney Fake Book – 2nd Edition

Over 200 of the most beloved songs of all time, including: Be Our Guest • Can You Feel the Love Tonight • Colors of the Wind • Cruella De Vil • Friend Like Me • Heigh-Ho • It's a Small World • Mickey Mouse March • Supercalifragilisticexpialidocious • Under the Sea • When You Wish upon a Star • A Whole New World • Zip-A-Dee-Doo-Dah • and more!

00240039 ....$27.95

The Folksong Fake Book

Over 1,000 folksongs perfect for performers, school teachers, and hobbyists. Includes: Bury Me Not on the Lone Prairie • Clementine • Danny Boy • The Erie Canal • Go, Tell It on the Mountain • Home on the Range • Kumbaya • Michael Row the Boat Ashore • Shenandoah • Simple Gifts • Swing Low, Sweet Chariot • When Johnny Comes Marching Home • Yankee Doodle • and many more.

00240151 ....$24.95

The Hymn Fake Book

Nearly 1,000 multi-denominational hymns perfect for church musicians or hobbyists: Amazing Grace • Christ the Lord Is Risen Today • For the Beauty of the Earth • It Is Well with My Soul • A Mighty Fortress Is Our God • O for a Thousand Tongues to Sing • Praise to the Lord, the Almighty • Take My Life and Let It Be • What a Friend We Have in Jesus • and hundreds more!

00240145 ....$24.95

The Praise & Worship Fake Book

400 songs: As the Deer • Better Is One Day • Come, Now Is the Time to Worship • Firm Foundation • Glorify Thy Name • Here I Am to Worship • I Could Sing of Your Love Forever • Lord, I Lift Your Name on High • More Precious Than Silver • Open the Eyes of My Heart • The Power of Your Love • Shine, Jesus, Shine • Trading My Sorrows • We Fall Down • You Are My All in All • and more.

00240234 $34.95

The R&B Fake Book – 2nd Edition

This terrific fake book features 375 classic R&B hits: Baby Love • Best of My Love • Dancing in the Street • Easy • Get Ready • Heatwave • Here and Now • Just Once • Let's Get It On • The Loco-Motion • (You Make Me Feel Like) A Natural Woman • One Sweet Day • Papa Was a Rollin' Stone • Save the Best for Last • September • Sexual Healing • Shop Around • Still • Tell It Like It Is • Up on the Roof • Walk on By • What's Going On • more!

00240107 C Edition $29.95

Ultimate Broadway Fake Book – 5th Edition

More than 700 show-stoppers from over 200 shows! Includes: Ain't Misbehavin' • All I Ask of You • Bewitched • Camelot • Don't Cry for Me Argentina • Edelweiss • I Dreamed a Dream • If I Were a Rich Man • Memory • Oklahoma • Send in the Clowns • What I Did for Love • more.

00240046 ....$49.99

FOR MORE INFORMATION, SEE YOUR LOCAL MUSIC DEALER, OR WRITE TO:

HAL•LEONARD® CORPORATION
7777 W. BLUEMOUND RD. P.O. BOX 13819 MILWAUKEE. WI 53213

Complete songlists available online at www.halleonard.com

Prices, contents and availabilty subject to change without notice.

The Ultimate Christmas Fake Book – 5th Edition

This updated edition includes 275 traditional and contemporary Christmas songs: Away in a Manger • The Christmas Song • Deck the Hall • Frosty the Snow Man • A Holly Jolly Christmas • I Heard the Bells on Christmas Day • Jingle Bells • Little Saint Nick • Merry Christmas, Darling • Nuttin' for Christmas • Rudolph the Red-Nosed Reindeer • Silent Night • What Child Is This? • more.

00240045 ....$24.95

The Ultimate Country Fake Book – 5th Edition

This book includes over 700 of your favorite country hits: Always on My Mind • Boot Scootin' Boogie • Crazy • Down at the Twist and Shout • Forever and Ever, Amen • Friends in Low Places • The Gambler • Jambalaya • King of the Road • Sixteen Tons • There's a Tear in My Beer • Your Cheatin' Heart • and hundreds more.

00240049 ....$49.99

The Ultimate Fake Book – 4th Edition

Includes over 1,200 hits: Blue Skies • Body and Soul • Endless Love • A Foggy Day • Isn't It Romantic? • Memory • Mona Lisa • Moon River • Operator • Piano Man • Roxanne • Satin Doll • Shout • Small World • Speak Softly, Love • Strawberry Fields Forever • Tears in Heaven • Unforgettable • hundreds more!

00240024 C Edition $49.95
00240026 B♭ Edition $49.95
00240025 E♭ Edition $49.95

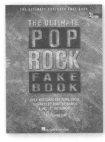

The Ultimate Pop/ Rock Fake Book – 4th Edition

Over 600 pop standards and contemporary hits, including: All Shook Up • Another One Bites the Dust • Crying • Don't Know Much • Dust in the Wind • Earth Angel • Every Breath You Take • Hero • Hey Jude • Hold My Hand • Imagine • Layla • The Loco-Motion • Oh, Pretty Woman • On Broadway • Spinning Wheel • Stand by Me • Stayin' Alive • Tears in Heaven • True Colors • The Twist • Vision of Love • A Whole New World • Wild Thing • Wooly Bully • Yesterday • more!

00240099 ....$39.99

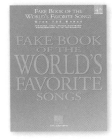

Fake Book of the World's Favorite Songs – 4th Edition

Over 700 favorites, including: America the Beautiful • Anchors Aweigh • Battle Hymn of the Republic • Bill Bailey, Won't You Please Come Home • Chopsticks • Für Elise • His Eye Is on the Sparrow • I Wonder Who's Kissing Her Now • Jesu, Joy of Man's Desiring • My Old Kentucky Home • Sidewalks of New York • Take Me Out to the Ball Game • When the Saints Go Marching In • and hundreds more!

00240072 ....$22.95

Presenting the Hal Leonard JAZZ PLAY-ALONG SERIES

For use with all B-flat, E-flat, Bass Clef and C instruments, the Jazz Play-Along® Series is the ultimate learning tool for all jazz musicians. With musician-friendly lead sheets, melody cues, and other split-track choices on the included CD, these first-of-a-kind packages help you master improvisation while playing some of the greatest tunes of all time. FOR STUDY, each tune includes a split track with: melody cue with proper style and inflection • professional rhythm tracks • choruses for soloing • removable bass part • removable piano part. FOR PERFORMANCE, each tune also has: an additional full stereo accompaniment track (no melody) • additional choruses for soloing.

1. DUKE ELLINGTON
00841644 .... $16.95

1A. MAIDEN VOYAGE/ALL BLUES
00843158 .... $15.99

2. MILES DAVIS
00841645 .... $16.95

3. THE BLUES
00841646 .... $16.99

4. JAZZ BALLADS
00841691 .... $16.99

5. BEST OF BEBOP
00841689 .... $16.99

6. JAZZ CLASSICS WITH EASY CHANGES
00841690 .... $16.99

7. ESSENTIAL JAZZ STANDARDS
00843000 .... $16.99

8. ANTONIO CARLOS JOBIM AND THE ART OF THE BOSSA NOVA
00843001 .... $16.95

9. DIZZY GILLESPIE
00843002 .... $16.99

10. DISNEY CLASSICS
00843003 .... $16.99

11. RODGERS AND HART FAVORITES
00843004 .... $16.99

12. ESSENTIAL JAZZ CLASSICS
00843005 .... $16.99

13. JOHN COLTRANE
00843006 .... $16.95

14. IRVING BERLIN
00843007 .... $15.99

15. RODGERS & HAMMERSTEIN
00843008 .... $15.99

16. COLE PORTER
00843009 .... $15.95

17. COUNT BASIE
00843010 .... $16.95

18. HAROLD ARLEN
00843011 .... $15.95

19. COOL JAZZ
00843012 .... $15.95

20. CHRISTMAS CAROLS
00843080 .... $14.95

21. RODGERS AND HART CLASSICS
00843014 .... $14.95

22. WAYNE SHORTER
00843015 .... $16.95

23. LATIN JAZZ
00843016 .... $16.95

24. EARLY JAZZ STANDARDS
00843017 .... $14.95

25. CHRISTMAS JAZZ
00843018 .... $16.95

26. CHARLIE PARKER
00843019 .... $16.95

27. GREAT JAZZ STANDARDS
00843020 .... $15.99

28. BIG BAND ERA
00843021 .... $15.99

29. LENNON AND MCCARTNEY
00843022 .... $16.95

30. BLUES' BEST
00843023 .... $15.99

31. JAZZ IN THREE
00843024 .... $15.99

32. BEST OF SWING
00843025 .... $15.99

33. SONNY ROLLINS
00843029 .... $15.95

34. ALL TIME STANDARDS
00843030 .... $15.99

35. BLUESY JAZZ
00843031 .... $15.99

36. HORACE SILVER
00843032 .... $16.99

37. BILL EVANS
00843033 .... $16.95

38. YULETIDE JAZZ
00843034 .... $16.95

39. "ALL THE THINGS YOU ARE" & MORE JEROME KERN SONGS
00843035 .... $15.99

40. BOSSA NOVA
00843036 .... $15.99

41. CLASSIC DUKE ELLINGTON
00843037 .... $16.99

42. GERRY MULLIGAN FAVORITES
00843038 .... $16.99

43. GERRY MULLIGAN CLASSICS
00843039 .... $16.95

44. OLIVER NELSON
00843040 .... $16.95

45. JAZZ AT THE MOVIES
00843041 .... $15.99

46. BROADWAY JAZZ STANDARDS
00843042 .... $15.99

47. CLASSIC JAZZ BALLADS
00843043 .... $15.99

48. BEBOP CLASSICS
00843044 .... $16.99

49. MILES DAVIS STANDARDS
00843045 .... $16.95

50. GREAT JAZZ CLASSICS
00843046 .... $15.99

51. UP-TEMPO JAZZ
00843047 .... $15.99

52. STEVIE WONDER
00843048 .... $15.95

53. RHYTHM CHANGES
00843049 .... $15.99

54. "MOONLIGHT IN VERMONT" AND OTHER GREAT STANDARDS
00843050 .... $15.99

55. BENNY GOLSON
00843052 .... $15.95

56. "GEORGIA ON MY MIND" & OTHER SONGS BY HOAGY CARMICHAEL
00843056 ....$15.99

57. VINCE GUARALDI
00843057 ....$16.99

58. MORE LENNON AND MCCARTNEY
00843059 ....$15.99

59. SOUL JAZZ
00843060 ....$15.99

60. DEXTER GORDON
00843061 ....$15.95

61. MONGO SANTAMARIA
00843062 ....$15.95

62. JAZZ-ROCK FUSION
00843063 ....$14.95

63. CLASSICAL JAZZ
00843064 ....$14.95

64. TV TUNES
00843065 ....$14.95

65. SMOOTH JAZZ
00843066 ....$16.99

66. A CHARLIE BROWN CHRISTMAS
00843067 ....$16.99

67. CHICK COREA
00843068 ....$15.95

68. CHARLES MINGUS
00843069 ....$16.95

69. CLASSIC JAZZ
00843071 ....$15.99

70. THE DOORS
00843072 ....$14.95

71. COLE PORTER CLASSICS
00843073 ....$14.95

72. CLASSIC JAZZ BALLADS
00843074 ....$15.99

73. JAZZ/BLUES
00843075 ....$14.95

74. BEST JAZZ CLASSICS
00843076 ....$15.99

75. PAUL DESMOND
00843077 ....$14.95

76. BROADWAY JAZZ BALLADS
00843078 ....$15.99

77. JAZZ ON BROADWAY
00843079 ....$15.99

78. STEELY DAN
00843070 ....$14.99

79. MILES DAVIS CLASSICS
00843081 ....$15.99

80. JIMI HENDRIX
00843083 ....$15.99

81. FRANK SINATRA – CLASSICS
00843084 ....$15.99

82. FRANK SINATRA – STANDARDS
00843085 ....$15.99

83. ANDREW LLOYD WEBBER
00843104 ....$14.95

84. BOSSA NOVA CLASSICS
00843105 ....$14.95

85. MOTOWN HITS
00843109 ....$14.95

86. BENNY GOODMAN
00843110 ....$14.95

87. DIXIELAND
00843111 ....$14.95

88. DUKE ELLINGTON FAVORITES
00843112 ....$14.95

89. IRVING BERLIN FAVORITES
00843113 ....$14.95

90. THELONIOUS MONK CLASSICS
00841262 ....$16.99

91. THELONIOUS MONK FAVORITES
00841263 ....$16.99

92. LEONARD BERNSTEIN
00450134 ....$15.99

93. DISNEY FAVORITES
00843142 ....$14.99

94. RAY
00843143 ....$14.99

95. JAZZ AT THE LOUNGE
00843144 ....$14.99

96. LATIN JAZZ STANDARDS
00843145 ....$14.99

97. MAYBE I'M AMAZED
00843148 ....$15.99

98. DAVE FRISHBERG
00843149 ....$15.99

99. SWINGING STANDARDS
00843150 ....$14.99

100. LOUIS ARMSTRONG
00740423 ....$15.99

101. BUD POWELL
00843152 ....$14.99

102. JAZZ POP
00843153 ....$14.99

103. ON GREEN DOLPHIN STREET & OTHER JAZZ CLASSICS
00843154 ....$14.99

104. ELTON JOHN
00843155 ....$14.99

105. SOULFUL JAZZ
00843151 ....$15.99

106. SLO' JAZZ
00843117 ....$14.99

107. MOTOWN CLASSICS
00843116 ....$14.99

108. JAZZ WALTZ
00843159 ....$15.99

109. OSCAR PETERSON
00843160 ....$15.99

110. JUST STANDARDS
00843161 ....$15.99

111. COOL CHRISTMAS
00843162 ....$15.99

114. MODERN JAZZ QUARTET FAVORITES
00843163 ....$15.99

115. THE SOUND OF MUSIC
00843164 ....$15.99

116. JACO PASTORIUS
00843165 ....$15.99

117. ANTONIO CARLOS JOBIM – MORE HITS
00843166 ....$15.99

118. BIG JAZZ STANDARDS COLLECTION
00843167 ....$27.50

119. JELLY ROLL MORTON
00843168 ....$15.99

120. J.S. BACH
00843169 ....$15.99

121. DJANGO REINHARDT
00843170 ....$15.99

122. PAUL SIMON
00843182 ....$16.99

123. BACHARACH & DAVID
00843185 ....$15.99

124. JAZZ-ROCK HORN HITS
00843186 ....$15.99

126. COUNT BASIE CLASSICS
00843157 ....$15.99

Prices, contents, and availability subject to change without notice.

FOR MORE INFORMATION,
SEE YOUR LOCAL MUSIC DEALER,
OR WRITE TO:

HAL•LEONARD®
CORPORATION
7777 W. BLUEMOUND RD. P.O. BOX 13819
MILWAUKEE, WISCONSIN 53213

For complete songlists and more,
visit Hal Leonard online at
www.halleonard.com

0910